SLANT SIX

ERIN BELIEU
SLANT SIX

 Copper Canyon Press
Port Townsend, Washington

Copper Canyon Press is in residence at Fort Worden State Park in Port
Townsend, Washington, under the auspices of Centrum. Centrum is a
gathering place for artists and creative thinkers from around the world,
students of all ages and backgrounds, and audiences seeking extraordinary
cultural enrichment.

LIBRARY OF CONGRESS CATALOGING-IN-PUBLICATION DATA

Belieu, Erin, 1965–
[Poems. Selections]
Slant Six / Erin Belieu.
    pages   cm
ISBN 978-1-55659-471-7 (paperback)
I. Title.
PS3552.E479A6 2014
813'.6—dc23

2014015971

9 8 7 6 5 4 3 2 FIRST PRINTING
COPPER CANYON PRESS
Post Office Box 271
Port Townsend, Washington 98368
www.coppercanyonpress.org

This book is for Adam Boles and Jude Countryman—

πᾶς γοῦν ποιητής γίγνεται οὗ ἂν Ἔρως ἅψηται

After this deluge
I wish to see the dove
saved,
nothing but the dove.

I would drown in this sea
if it did not fly away,
if it did not return with the leaf
in the final hour.

"Nach dieser Sintflut," Ingeborg Bachmann

CONTENTS

SLANT SIX

ARS POETICA FOR THE FUTURE

The Rapture came
and went without incident,

but I put off folding my laundry,
just in case.

Also, from my inbox this morning,
subject header:

"Lesbian Torture Camps."
The mind ricochets like a fly—

is there anything left for people
to do to people?

Meanwhile, my boyfriend
looks forward to the apocalypse

as a retirement party
he pretends he won't be

attending, like the characters
in the movie who climb the highest

building, wanting to be the first
to welcome the spaceship.

In this world,

I've given up sleep for dreaming
and art is still our only flying car,

but I can't recall when anticipation
became the substitute for hope.

Recently, C. said, "Now we begin
the poems of our Great Middle Period."

I imagine digging a series of small
holes, burying poems in Ziploc

baggies. I imagine them as baby teeth
knocked from the present's mouth.

SOMEONE ASKS, WHAT MAKES THIS POEM AMERICAN?

And I answer by driving around, which seems
to me the most American of activities, up there
with waving the incendiary dandelion of sparklers
or eating potato salad with green specks of relish,
the German kind, salad of immigrants, of all
the strange, pickled things we carry
over from other places, like we did on Easter
mornings in Nebraska, stuffing our Sunday
shoes full of straw so that either Jesus
or the Easter Bunny could leave us small,
bullet-shaped candies in honor of what, I was
never quite sure. Where do such customs
come from? Everywhere!
      Americanness is everywhere,
wedged into everything, is best when driving
around a frowsy Gulf Coast city with its terrific
mini-marts like Bill's, the very best of all marts!
UN of toasted boat rats and boys from the projects
revving their hoopties; of biscuit-shaped ladies who
penny their scratch cards and hold up the line;
where Panama (from Panama) commands
the counter, and Mr. Bud, the camel-faced man,
offers every kid a sweetie, producing a jar
of petrified lollies from a shelf also

displaying an array of swirly glassed pipes
and Arthurian bongs, where Raul the Enforcer
idles at the back, packing since the incident
in the parking lot last summer.
                         Of course, people
here have their discontents: the artists save
what tips they don't snort and always mean
to leave for New York or Seattle, though I tell
them both drizzle like November half the time.
So I say, No! That's un-American. We need
our artists everywhere, not scrunched up
in one or two rarefied spots,
which makes their parties anxious. And Miłosz
says artists come from everywhere, from everyplace,
the capital *and* the provinces, to keep
the body healthy or else end up like 17th-
century Hapsburgs or German shepherds
listing with hip dysplasia. So I'm circling
the swampy taint of this Southern city, choosing
art, choosing to be American, actively pursuing
that fabled happiness when the alternatives
present themselves, which is my obligation,
both legislator and witness to Bill's
Mini-Mart and Mike's Chinese Grocery,
and the hungry citizens queuing up
in front of Jenny's Lunchbox, waiting
on line for a pile of cheese grits to start
this day, placing them firmly for the moment

in the happiness column. Because what's more
American than a full stomach on a sunny morning?
What more than this fat-assed acceleration,
driving with the windows cranked down?

LOVE IS NOT AN EMERGENCY

More like weather, that is,
ubiquitous, true
        or false spring—the ambivalence
we have
        for any picnic—

flies ass-up in the Jell-O,
        the soft bulge of thunderheads.

Right now, the man in the booth
next to me
        at the Nautilus Diner,
                Madison, New Jersey,

is crying, but looks up
        to order their famous disco fries.

So the world's saddest thing shakes you
        like a Magic 8 Ball;

and before him, the minstrel
        who smeared on love's blackface, rattling
his damage like a tambourine.

I have been the deadest nag
      limping circles round

the paddock, have flown to beady pieces,

sick as the tongue of mercury
      at the thermometer's tip.

But let's admit there's a pleasure, too,
in living as we do,

      like three-strike felons who smile
for the security cameras,

like love's first responders,

stuffing our kits with enhancement
      pills, Zig-Zags, and Powerball cards.

I read: *to greet* is the cognate for
      regret, to weep, but welcome
      our weeping,

because we "grant the name of love
      to something less than love,"

      because we all have to eat.

THE BODY IS A BIG SAGACITY

is another thing Nietzsche said
that hits me as pretty specious,
while sitting in my car in the Costco
parking lot, listening to the *Ballet
mécanique* of metal buggies shrieking,
as each super, singular, and self-contained
wisdom of this Monday morning rumbles
its jumbo packs of toilet paper and Diet Coke
up the sidewalk. So count me a Despiser
of the Body, though I didn't generate this
woe any more than the little man parked
next to me, now attempting the descent from
his giant truck, behemoth whose Hemi roars
like a melting reactor and stands
as the ego's corrective to the base methods
by which the body lets the spirit down.

Buzz-clipped, tidy as an otter, he's high and
tight in his riding heels. Pearl snaps on
the little man's shirt throw tiny lasers
when he passes. But who isn't more war
than peace? And how ridiculous to suffer
this: to be a little man, with itty hands
and bitty feet, to know yourself lethal, but

Krazy Glued for life to the most laughable
engine. Recycled, rewired, product of
genes and whatever our mamas thought
to smoke: the spirit gets no vote, Fred.

My body once was whole, symmetrical, was
actually beautiful for three consecutive years,
expensive as a rented palace, and yet I blew
that measly era watching my clock hands move,
as if I were the trigger rigged to homemade
dynamite. But if you would look inside me,
into all the lonely seeming folks here loading
their heavy bags, you'd hope we're something
more than a sack of impulse, of soul defined
by random gristle. Which is why the little man
pauses on the sidewalk, why he stops to look at
me looking at him: this pocket-size person,
whose gaze unkinks a low, hairy voltage from
my coccyx. And thus speaks Zarathustra,
        You Great Star,
what would Your happiness be
had You not those for whom
You shine?
        Ask the little man, neither ghost nor plant,
his bootheels ringing down the concrete.

I GROWED NO POTATOES TO WRITE ABOUT, SIR

nor bogs, nor fathers,
nor special water that was my place
alone to make me hard and wise—
I did not sow nor bury, nor even try to
fudge my nothings in such dirt with
much bestoried, peaty spade. My wars
were far away and fought by men (I fear)
I do not know. Hi ho. And hence to lady
work I went. A-sent, ago, long scrubbing at
my bits to strip them extra minty meadow
clean. And only then convened the Little
Ladies' Manners class. Of Sundays, played
me wormy rose, decaying that corsage
of girls pinned to spindly ballroom chairs
for lessons at our fancy luncheonette. Sir,
we were a pastel herd. When handed
us the rulers, be best assured we clenched
them tense between our knees. You mind
your Qs and Ps, Sir! We snapped our thighs
right shut, Sir. A hairy practice, to quick
the lady trap. But O! it made a vestal woe
to pay when rulers dropped, for those who
gived a skinful inch.

And so, from there
my lady life increased, soft balled, soft
voiced, with little tools to fit my box.
Do not tell, Sir, for we are friends, Sir.
Is that a yes? Then I will confess of nights
when tides are slapping me about, moon-
doodled as I am, and that betimes I creep
into your plot and choose your best and
biggest digger. Secret-like, I press the shaft
inside my knee. I strain until the blisters
come. Freely, Sir, without a word,
I dig. I score. I tamp your squelchy turf.

WHEN AT A CERTAIN PARTY IN NYC

Wherever you're from sucks,
and wherever you grew up sucks,
and everyone here lives in a converted
chocolate factory or deconsecrated church,
without an ugly lamp or souvenir coffee cup
in sight, but only carefully edited *objets* like
the Lacanian soap dispenser in the kitchen
that looks like an industrial-age dildo, and
when you rifle through the bathroom
looking for a spare tampon, you discover
that even their toothpaste is somehow more
desirable than yours. And later you go
with a world-famous critic to eat a plate
of sushi prepared by a world-famous chef from
Sweden and the roll is conceived to look like
"a strand of pearls around a white throat," and is
so confusingly beautiful that it makes itself
impossible to eat. And your friend back home—
who says the pioneers who first settled
the great asphalt parking lot of our
Middle, were not in fact heroic but, really,
the chubby ones who lacked the imagination
to go all the way to California—it could be that
she's onto something. Because, admit it,

when you look at the people on these streets,
the razor-blade women with their strategic bones
and the men wearing Amish pants with
interesting zippers, it's pretty clear that you
will never cut it anywhere that constitutes
a *where*, that even ordering a pint of tuna salad in
a deli is an illustrative exercise in self-doubt.
So when you see the dogs on the high-rise elevators
practically tweaking, panting all the way down
from the 19th floor to the 1st, dying to get on
with their long-planned business of snuffling
trash or peeing on something to which all day
they've been looking forward, what you want is
to be on the fastest Conestoga home, where the other
losers live and where the tasteless azaleas are,
as we speak, halfheartedly exploding.

H. RES. 21-1: PROPOSING THE BAN OF PUSH-UP BRAS, ETC.

So it goes:
the foundation drops
        and the ladies are busted,
                those old carpetbaggers
        slouching south.
                O America,
we don't mean to disappoint,
        but every lover comes
with a fulsome jiggle,
some pudding
        packed in the U-Haul,
                a mole we want to believe
could be viewed as a beauty mark.
        But honestly,
isn't the honeymoon
        the boring part?
                All that lying about!
And what is beauty but
        the absence of symmetry?
Better to forget
        perfection, to remember
                we were born a nation of
blemishes, a posse of strays
        with cellulite.

If Benjamin Franklin
     were alive today, you know
          he'd be working a thong and
Rollerblades on Venice Beach,
     flying his freak flag
          just beneath Old Glory!
America, it's time
     to unsuck those bellies
          and show our ugly asses.
     We must learn
to want each other
          in direct sunlight,
no more or less than
     what we really are.

HOW WE COUNT IN THE SOUTH

       Add one
tonight, when the barred owl
calls her tent revival, the cortege
trailing a mosquito truck's
deodorant breeze.
       Plus two, the night
before, where they inject one more
black man up the road in Georgia.
The Supreme Court tweets his final
opinion.
       Which leads to three:
Dear Jesus, the Reason
for Each Season, of course we're
exhausted by our souls' litigation;
the old ones still milling at the polling
place, the recently deceased sweating
their subpoenas in feckless hands.
       Required to appear,
we wait. We nurse ourselves and take
a number. We lean against the sneeze
guard at the country buffet until our
ankles swell.
       Please. Don't tell us
history. Nobody hearts a cemetery

like we do,
        where reenactors bite
their bullets between headstones,
and ancient belles in neck-high silk
prepare for the previously fought
war. Every day is a day before.
            Though we do hear
the news. Oh sure. It gets to us.
Story is, up north, people shit
crushed pineapple and rest-stop
whores make change with paper
money. Story is
        inscribed, fixed as
the roulette wheels clacking inside
casinos, where party boats freak
like viscous bath toys in this
electric gulf.
        Certainly, we've learned
our numbers. We build a church for
anyone who owns a pair of knees.
But still, the old disease is catching,
        so pray with us—
            Unplug the power, Lord.
        Illuminate the devils. Degrease
                the righteous man's eye.

))

12-STEP

I am considering
lighthouses

in a completely new light—

their butch neutrality, their grand
but modest surfaces.

A lighthouse could appear
here at any moment.

I have been making this effort,
placing myself in uncomfortable positions,

only for the documented health benefits.

I believe there is a helping of vegetables
in every selfless and measured thought.

I am now able to hold subjects—
like lighthouses—at an objective angle

and admire them for their spooky,
correlative truths.

Despite past evidence and gratuitous use
of the first person,

I do wish to improve.

Each day I start anew, launching myself
against the great sea of

myself,

though my dinghy is not
in any way personal.

There is a very real lighthouse
in my future.

I must change
what I cannot accept.

PERFECT

is not what I was,
though you said I was,

in an apartment in St. Louis
on a green shag carpet redolent
of the previous renter's cat.
Above all things, I am accurate.

So what to say of the sunlight?
Nothing.

In the 21st century, there's nothing
to say about sunlight which lasted
as long as it takes to have sex, and
made us feel as warm as humans get,

perfectly human, perfectly warm,
though, sadly, you don't remember this.

Though, sadly, I remember this, and
it still makes me angry—
which is another word for *sad*
as well as a synonym for *nothing*.

Though if anything is,
your sadness is perfect,

your human disappointment,
which you've raised like a baby
in a black BabyBjörn,
coaxing it into the best sadness

anything warm could hope for.
Your sadness gets a perfect score,
a 1600 on the GRE.
But if I had a gun,

I'd shoot your sadness through
the knee. Then the head.

Or if I were a goddess,
I'd turn you to a tree with silver leaves

or a flower with a center as yellow as
sunlight, like they used to do when saving

the beautiful from themselves.

BURYING IT

There's an old man I know
who lives in a TV-sized house

with one window.

There's an old man I know
who has one smeared window

through which he cannot see.

I know that window is the ghoul
of a window, crazed all over

like filigree. I know it like
the caged hamster knows,

the furry things handled
                until they give.

꜒)

You made up a science project,
a weather balloon—

so I ran through our streets
with a huge plastic bag trailing behind me,

transparent, shaped like a giant
used condom. Oh, we never cared
what anyone thought! We were

those kind of people.

That was so funny.

Me running and running,
filling it with wind
that wouldn't get in.

           ꙮ)

I know an old man who's afraid
to eat. If you touch him,

bruises appear everywhere
like blood carnations. He is emotional,
but only in traffic. He has a window
that clings to its frame

like shatter glass after an accident.

If you moved,
the whole thing would run to liquid.

Glass is like that.
Glass is always looking

for a reason.
It would be best for everyone

       to hold very still.

   ))

Did you know honeysuckles look like wasps
if you look at them?

My son told me that.

My son sees everything because
he's close to the ground.

My son sees everything

but pretends to need glasses. Why does he pretend
to need glasses?

That's a kid mystery. The blindness you have,
they want it, too.

My son finds the shine

people lose in the weeds and
he gives it to me.

))

Remember that day at the Mormon cemetery
and you filming me running over the graves—

did I make that up?

You, with your special camera that cut time
into pieces.

And the statue of the pioneer couple
burying their stone baby.

They caught bubonic plague and died,
all the stone people.

Poor baby.

You were making a filmstrip. I'm the girl
in it, running over the graves.

OLENTANGY RIVER

Hardest day   ever   in Ohio: and gray
and coldest   as if there were   another day
in Ohio   as if   the sun

that spelled   briefly where   we walked
for   hours   freezing   were a magic   as I
needed   it to be: golem's proof   and
yenta's blessing   to those   many nights
of driving   past   your house:

inexorable   self   embarrassed   fuller
than   an itch   something better than   this
sore   those nights   not knowing   where
exactly   but inevitable   and clearly set

on   a direction   that place   where I was
driving   because   of course   there   was you
somewhere   sleeping   or   toasting bread   or
staring   tired at   TV: and ending lost   always

lost: still   you've never been   imagined   as
I   imagined   you: today   with a wife   sleeping
in Ohio   and babies   down the hall   not ever
so   reached for: what did you do?   There by
the Olentangy   once called   *stone   for its knife*

and *therefore my soul   caught   at the place*
which is fitting   whetted   as I was   and
sudden   in Ohio   where objects   are steep
to climb   and wrong: but you   walking

with your   Herbert   this gift   a little
nothing   what you offered   on my shelf
now   hand whitening   in the freezing   and

you   ungloved: and there   your voice
always   where   we are walking   will always
be   walking   by the Olentangy   freezing.

FATHERS NEVER ANSWER

A basket in the shape of
a sunflower—

still hanging on
your bedroom wall.

You made it in school.

You loved it so much
you wouldn't stop

making it. Or couldn't
stop. We never agree

on what you said.
But I was your favorite.

I thought, What kind of boy
makes such a basket?

Professional-looking, all
tight and golden, hanging

on your bedroom wall.
You said

you couldn't stop
making it, weaving it—

however it is you
make a basket—

or wouldn't stop. Even
when they threatened

you with a school for
"retarded boys,"

because you didn't
stop. This was back

then, when parents
said things like that.

A different story, what
we used to do.

But I never forgot.

I thought, Remarkable.
Why wouldn't he

just stop?

VICTORIA STATION

When a girl is the disaster,

mostly minor, the thing gone
wonky before even attempted,
too sticky to clean;

the obvious, unsolvable,
an appliance with directions
lost in the junk drawer. When

a wreck, red-haired,
red-faced, this clown of a girl,
unfunny, is urgent as the red-

lacquered phone box
she bawls into weekly, fears
herself the character

whose paragraphs you skip—

        then the tea shop
outside Victoria Station,
cologne of pears wicking from

the door. Then the fleur-de-lis
of freesia bunched at every
table where ladies idle in

sturdy skirts. A shelter,

all quiet, a shop with an owner
who sets a girl down, weightless,
a cup, transparently boned.

Who never knows kindness
will be a map: the scent of pears
and freesia, white stones

on a path, the driftwood
she clings to when disguised as
a beggar, this girl asleep

on the hero's beach.

TIME MACHINE

Perceptions and memories become tinged
with an indefinable quality, as with a kind of heat
or light, so novel that now and then, as we stare
at our own self, we wonder how it can really exist.

Time and Free Will, Henri Bergson

Commit Random Acts of Kindness
is what the bumper sticker says
on the Volvo that cuts me off
in traffic, driven by a woman
      who then gives me the finger.
And without even meaning to,
she builds a functioning time machine,
defying the laws of physics!
Spark of Wells's dream and Vonnegut's
slaughter, this genius device she's made,
bringing present to past and past to
future. With one skinny digit, she flips
a lever that busts me down to my
molecules, dissolved like the salt
in a ramen packet;
      because now I'm whooshing
through the continuum, weightless as
a deposit slip in a bank's pneumatic
tube, no longer composed as me,

a middle-aged person eating sushi
off the seat of a Volkswagen sedan,
late to fetch my son from school. Instead,
            here she is, my former self,
unseen for twenty years.
                    Who *is* this girl?
In the rearview, I look pretty
unpromising, a state-school scrub,
the missing link of thrift-store chic.
And no matter the dimension,
I'm late for work, racing to
the record store where bong hits are
corporate policy and Christian Death's
Only Theatre of Pain is racked under
"Gospel." Of course,
I recall: this other *me,*
this place, this day, this mostly
unsympathetic girl, who doesn't know
how soon she'll be fired for sleeping
with the boss.
            And it's now, in this moment,
when the backflow of time and my
immediate NOW-ness are fusing
together, I know
                    what comes next —
the *other* finger:
casual, infamous, locked these years
in the gulag of my memory, *that* finger,

but attached to a different woman—
she in her silver Mercedes, who,
by the rule of time travel, blows through
this heavy traffic, forcing me off
the road. Again.
    In this past universe,
she's right on time, still looking chilled,
vacuum-sealed, cool as an aspic
served at a benefit luncheon with
a garnish I wouldn't know not to eat.
The woman in her silver Mercedes
has returned to flip me this same
snide salute, both rank and rancor
etched in her gesture.
    And where could I be
but in my beat Plymouth Duster,
muscle of Bondo and bad intentions,
mine for the three hundred dollars
it's taken this year to save?
    Time unspools, and here I sit,
road-rashed, knotted in the service
ditch of my humiliation,
snagged in the past, which is present,
thinking, *It should be harder to feel
this angry all the time.*

    That I should be embarrassed
by what happens next:
swerving back to the road, I make it

my mission to *stalk this bitch*
in her silver Mercedes, roaring
once more through creamy suburbs,
hunting her down cul-de-sacs
with careful lawns, their safety
the illusion I think I will never buy.

    In future, do I call this a moment
of satisfaction? Find it righteous?
My Slant-6 gunning up her tailpipe;
the *Wild Kingdom* death scene
of her composure as she scrambles
to get away?

             And then, midchase,
I'm out, lifted bodily, back to being
this person of a certain age, my semi-
luxury sedan, takeout warming on
the seat. I'm back, where the woman
and her bumper sticker are now
turning left.

    This world resumes.
At the light, we wait to move
along. And yes,
why wouldn't we? For this woman
in her Volvo, I don't equal a flea
on the ass of a thought anymore.

    Commit Random Acts of Kindness
is what the bumper sticker says.
I recall I'm late to get my son.

Blink blink,
goes her signal,
            blink blink.

THE PROBLEM OF THE DOMESTIC

Should be easier this morning
since you've kept me up all night
with your allergy attack,

forgetting to take your pill
until it's too late
and petting the cat because
you're a stooge for her slutty ways,
letting her sleep on your lap when
you know you shouldn't.

And there's me, knowing soon
you'll wake up and come find me

      here, in the garage,

where I'm smoking and trying
to write a poem in which you appear,
to peevishly announce we need
to quit smoking while reaching for
the pack. But even this perfectly

annoying entrance is bad for
business:
      Who better than you,

topless in your plaid pajama pants
which are, as ever, turned inside out?

And to those who'd say
there's worse than the trouble
of an irritated man standing hairy
in the January grace of

a fine north Florida morning—
        kudos to you for knowing
what I'm talking about.

ENERGY POLICY

This practical kid, born
Capricorn, actuary of the stars,

he's planning my death,
sure of the thermodynamic heaven

he's invented. Because energy
must go somewhere in this system,

in his, I'll be repurposed as a tree.
And this comforts me, as no churchy

coupons for paradise ever could.
Finally fitting, I'll meet my zero as

the absolute, container of soot buried
at a sapling's root. An organized boy,

he considers all options, what tree to
choose. I haggle for the ornamental—

jazz hands of a jacaranda,
firethorn to match my hair—

but am dismissed.
He insists on something sturdy:

What lives forever? Then, revising,
Or closest to? Next comes

the issue of where, harder
to answer as sequoias don't grow in

Nebraska. *Let's put,* he says, *a pin
in that.* It's his meeting, so we move

on to scenarios, the portrait he'll nail
to my trunk, a bench to sit on when

he comes to talk with me. But what kind
of bench? There's much to discuss with

this faithful child, who knows better than
to bet on the equilibrium, watching

ice in his glass, disordered by degree,
the first shareholder in my entropy.

))

WITH BIRDS

It's all *Romeo and Juliet*—

hate crimes, booty calls, political
assassinations.

Who's more Tybalt than the blue jay?
More Mercutio than the mockingbird?

That ibis pretending to be a lawn ornament
makes a vain and stupid prince.

Birds living in their city-states, flinging
mob hits from the sky, they drop their dead

half-chewed at my gates. But give anything

even one lice-riddled wing, and suddenly
we're symbolic, in league with the adult

collector of teddy bears, the best-addressed-
in-therapy pinned like a kitty-cat calendar in

every cubicle. Pathetic, really. With birds,
make no exception.

                    Alright. It's possible
I'll give you this morning's

mourning doves, there on the telephone
wire, apart from the hoi polloi—

something in their pink, the exact shade
of an aubade. And shouldn't we recall

that keen, pheromonal terror, when dawn
arrives too bright, too soon? Let's hope we

never muster what God put in the goose's
head. For this, you keep the doves.

"A ROTTENNESS BEGINS IN HIS CONDUCT"

The candidate has
a spoilage in his head,

an icky bit, a creep
that chews for him alone
when stuffing up the local

grub. At every stop,
he shovels in the pies and
dogs, the beer, the dough.

Our candidate,

he makes himself, he
takes the extra pump
of cheese. Not easy

as you please, to keep it
down, handed what
you're given. And so

we are. But so is he!
Alike, who isn't driven
far to serve? But dread

is what he's said or done,
the condiment atop
a weakened thing

you'll come to know,
to know exactly who
our candidate's become.

Or will. Was never
what he meant. Or,

maybe not. Tonight,
it's comfy here:
you, me, the worm—

we've got our snacks.
Let's spoon. We'll see
what's on TV.

POEM OF PHILOSOPHICAL AND PARENTAL CONUNDRUMS
WRITTEN IN AN ELECTION YEAR

From the backseat, Jude saying, Mama, I HATE
Republicans, and the way he says HATE,
saying it the way only a seven-year-old can,

saying it like he's very, very certain,

is plenty disturbing since I've never once
heard the word HATE come out of his mouth
until this morning. And there are those

who may be reading this poem,
those people without children, or
those, I should say, who choose not
to have children, you might be impatient

now that Jude has appeared here to make
his meaningful pronouncement, and I
get how tedious it is, listening to those

who choose to have children
drone on about the stupidity of standardized
tests and the difficulty in finding authentically
organic apple juice; but I beg your patience and

ask you to imagine how unnerving it is to be
responsible for these weird beings who rarely
do anything you'd expected when you were
reading *What to Expect When You're Expecting;*

how we're suckered into thinking this kid stuff
is a science when really it's the most abstract
art form, like you're standing in a gallery at

MoMA, staring at an aquarium in which float
three basketballs, and the piece is titled
Aquarium with Three Basketballs,

and you're looking at the others in the gallery
considering the basketballs and *they* don't look
as if they're having some eye-crossing internal
struggle, and you're sweating a little

and embarrassed, thinking,
There's a message here that I'm not getting,

which is what it feels like, often, to have a child,
and what I ponder in this moment: whether I've
blown it again, as Jude, nicknamed by his teachers

"The Radiating Joy Machine," boy of peculiar light
and unusual kindness, has arrived this morning
in the backseat of the car, belting out the word
HATE and sounding like he absolutely means it.

And there are more practical difficulties beyond
what could be viewed as the self-indulgently
philosophical, such as Jude's father, my ex-husband,

who's given me a speech the day before about
not pushing our politics on Jude and letting him
make up his own mind when he's old enough
to understand the complexities of the issues.

And, on principle, surely, I agree,

though I know another factor must be
that Jude's father is now married to a woman
who's half Cuban and from Miami, who's not

thrilled with Jude piping up about Republicans and
booing every time a GOP candidate appears on TV.

And that's what you call the *realpolitik* in action
when it comes to divorce, wherein the rubber hits
the "blended" family's road. But since I'm not

half Cuban and not from Miami, I don't pretend I
can speak to the cultural pressure and loyalties of
the single-issue voter, though secretly I want to say

to my ex-husband, the die-hardest of liberals —
something I'll always love about him — I want to say,

Really? When your beloved aunt is gay, as is my
brother, whose husband is a political exile from
Colombia? When Jude has a medical issue that

might someday be cured by stem cell therapy,
as insurance drains our paychecks every month
while refusing to pay for a single, useful thing?

Really? But deep down, I know he's right. If Jude
has come to HATE, it's probably come through
me, even though I try so hard to love the sinner

even when the sin is the most fucockulous
interpretation of the Old Testament
that makes me want to grab every Christian
evangelical by the neck and shake them till their

brains kick in. Which makes me think of my friend
Matt, a boy I had a crush on in high school, who's
now a corporate attorney in Houston; Matt,

who's tracked me down on the Internet and we've
taken to flaming each other about politics by e-mail;
how recently he sent me his beautiful family's
Christmas card, and honestly they don't *look* evil,

and Matt says he'd rather choose whom to help with
his money than have it flushed on social programs

that clearly don't work. And while he doesn't convince
me, I grudgingly acknowledge this point of view and

concede that not all Republicans, even tax attorneys
in Texas, are necessarily Earth-raping titans
with $7,000 shower curtains, that they may have
actual convictions, holding them as dearly as

I do my own. So finally, I tell Jude we might
STRONGLY DISAGREE with people's opinions,
but we try to love the people themselves. Then I
tell him briefly about a guy named Gandhi and
another guy named Martin Luther King and how

the progressive mind always triumphs in the end,
and he's maybe paying attention, though he's tricky
that way and glazes over often, as you can imagine.

But he's satisfied for the moment, squinting through
the foggy car window, and I feel better as it's morning,
with the sun just poking up over the canopied road

as we drive quietly through our tidy neighborhood
of houses with doorway flags promoting pineapples
and football teams and whatever else my neighbors

feel the need to advertise, and I'm thinking
maybe I got it right this time,

maybe I did okay at least; this doesn't have to
be the thing Jude talks about someday in therapy.

But with kids, you never know,
as our present is busy becoming
their future, every minute, every day,

while they're working as hard as they can
to perfect the obstinate and beautiful mystery
that every soul ends up being to every other.

LOVE LETTER: FINAL VISITATION

I come back to you
in the interregnum of wisteria,
   in the epoch of the armadillo's
fetching leprosy: storm season, mold season, season of
Savannah's ghosts rotting for
   the sozzled gawkers. Parked in
the public fountains, your banshees rattle
their Marley chains, carry signs that read
   Will Work for Any
     Human Sympathy.
   But there's none left over:
we blew, we consumed, we squandered, we lavished,
we bounced that check high as a Super Ball and snickered
as it leapt away.
     O, we were numb, dumb, and increasingly
wasted; put pigs in the Piggly Wiggly, did ravage
and damage. We read the infected stories, mumbled them
high at the lip of the Devil's Pool. What is a kiss
   but the mouth's potential for wreckage?

   I come back to you: yes,
     wept for, wracked, and now unfamiliar—
the cauldron's cold in the shed and I can't
put a hand to my planchette, no matter where

I look. Peace, peace, I free and undream you.
    The priestess of nothing,
        I am pleased to be plain.

FIELD

Field is pause   field is plot   field is red chigger bump where
the larvae feed   corn wig curled in your ear. Field cares not
a fig for your resistance   though kindly   gently   *lay your
head down   girl   lay it down.*   When ready   storm   when
summer   kilned smoothly as a cake. Awake! Awake and
wide is field. And viral. Biotic. Field of patience   of percolation
and policy. Your human energy. Come again? What for? In
field   there is no time at all   no use   a relief   the effort done
which is   thank you   finally   the very lack of you.   *Lay your
head down   girl   lay it down.*   In field   which has waited since
you first ascended to the raw end of your squared-off world and
gazed upon your subjects: majesty of rat snake   corn snake
of all the low ribbons bandaging the stalks. Progress in field
foot sliding in matter   slick chaff in fall.   And always   field's oboe
this sawing   a wind   that is drawing its nocturne through the 23rd
mansion of the moon. Field   is Requiel's music and the Wild Hunt
of offer. In field   they are waiting   you are sounding. Go home.

APRÈS MOI

is pest, is plague, is
global atrophy, desire
insipid, the single
saltine in its crumpled
sleeve. Future of
courtesy balance and
hysterical number,
markets depressed,
a bottomed-out
GDP.
      Oh yes,
it all goes up.
Kablooey! Good luck
enjoying those bonfires
with no s'mores!
      Big, BIG
mistake, to make this
life without me. So
when the horsemen
descend on your
address, ride jiggety
clop to your
empty door,
      you

can explain this mess.
I won't live here
anymore. To you,
I bequeath a world
where cupboards stick,
with nothing left
to creak for.

NOTES

Dedication from Plato: "Love makes poets of us all."

"Nach dieser Sintflut" was translated by Johannes Beilharz.

"Ars Poetica for the Future" is for Joshua Beckman. I promised him a poem with a flying car in it some years ago.

In "Love Is Not an Emergency," the line "grant the name of love to something less than love" comes from Gina Berriault's short story "The Infinite Passion of Expectation." This poem is for Ashley Capps.

The Nietzsche quotes in "The Body Is a Big Sagacity" are from the "Prologue" and the fourth speech of *Thus Spoke Zarathustra*.

"When at a Certain Party in NYC" is for Mark Bibbins and Brian Chambers.

The line "therefore my soul caught at the place" in "Olentangy River" is a slight paraphrasing of a line in George Herbert's poem "Affliction (I)."

"Time Machine" is for Andrew Missel and Jennine Capó Crucet, and inspired by Robert Pinsky's school of courteous driving habits.

"The Problem of the Domestic" is for Adam Boles. By any means necessary, darling.

"When once a man has cast a longing eye on [offices], a rottenness begins in his conduct" is from a letter Thomas Jefferson wrote to Tench Coxe in 1799.

As always, my thanks to the excellent posse of good friends—both poet and civilian—who helped me with this book along the way.

ABOUT THE AUTHOR

Erin Belieu is the author of four poetry collections, including *Infanta, One Above & One Below,* and *Black Box,* all from Copper Canyon Press. She has been selected for the National Poetry Series, is recipient of a Rona Jaffe Foundation fellowship, a Breadloaf fellowship, the Ohioana Book Award, and the Midlands Author Award, and was a finalist for the Los Angeles Times Book Prize. Her work has appeared in *The New Yorker, The New York Times, The Atlantic, Ploughshares, Slate,* and *The Best American Poetry.* Belieu teaches in the writing program at Florida State University and the low-residency MFA program at Lesley University in Cambridge, Massachussetts. She is also the co-founder and director of the organization VIDA: Women in Literary Arts and is artistic director for the Port Townsend Writers' Conference. Belieu lives in Tallahassee, Florida.

ACKNOWLEDGMENTS

Acknowledgment goes to the magazines in which these poems first appeared (sometimes in different versions):

Academy of American Poets' *Poem-A-Day:* "Field"; *The Awl:* "Ars Poetica for the Future"; *The Cincinnati Review:* "Olentangy River"; *Conversations Across Borders:* "How We Count in the South"; *The Cortland Review:* "Time Machine"; *LIT:* "Poem of Philosophical and Parental Conundrums Written in an Election Year"; *The Literary Review:* "A Rottenness Begins in His Conduct"; *Lo-Ball:* "Burying It"; *The New Guard:* "Love Letter: Final Visitation"; *The New Yorker:* "Après Moi"; *The Normal School:* "With Birds"; *Ploughshares:* "The Body Is a Big Sagacity," "Energy Policy," "Fathers Never Answer," "Someone Asks, What Makes This Poem American?"; *Prairie Schooner:* "The Problem of the Domestic," "12-Step"; *The Rumpus:* "I Growed No Potatoes To Write About, Sir"; *Slate:* "Love Is Not an Emergency"; *32 Poems:* "When at a Certain Party in NYC"; *Willow Springs:* "Perfect."

"When at a Certain Party in NYC" appears in *The Best American Poetry 2011.*

"With Birds" appears in *The Best American Poetry 2014.*

"Victoria Station" appears in the anthology *The Book of Scented Things.*

"H. Res. 21-1: Proposing the Ban of Push-Up Bras, Etc." appears in the anthology *Starting Today: 100 Poems for Obama's First 100 Days.*

Poetry is vital to language and living. Since 1972, Copper Canyon Press has published extraordinary poetry from around the world to engage the imaginations and intellects of readers, writers, booksellers, librarians, teachers, students, and donors.

WE ARE GRATEFUL FOR THE MAJOR SUPPORT PROVIDED BY:

THE PAUL G. ALLEN
FAMILY FOUNDATION

Lannan

THE MAURER FAMILY
FOUNDATION

ART WORKS.
National Endowment for the Arts
arts.gov

A&
OFFICE OF ARTS & CULTURE
SEATTLE

WASHINGTON STATE
ARTS COMMISSION

Anonymous

John Branch

Diana Broze

Beroz Ferrell & The Point, LLC

Janet and Les Cox

Mimi Gardner Gates

Gull Industries, Inc.
on behalf of William and Ruth True

Linda Gerrard and Walter Parsons

Mark Hamilton and Suzie Rapp

Carolyn and Robert Hedin

Steven Myron Holl

Lakeside Industries, Inc.
on behalf of Jeanne Marie Lee

Maureen Lee and Mark Busto

Brice Marden

Ellie Mathews and Carl Youngmann as
The North Press

H. Stewart Parker

Penny and Jerry Peabody

John Phillips and Anne O'Donnell

Joseph C. Roberts

Cynthia Lovelace Sears and Frank Buxton

The Seattle Foundation

Dan Waggoner

Charles and Barbara Wright

The dedicated interns and faithful volunteers of Copper Canyon Press

TO LEARN MORE ABOUT UNDERWRITING COPPER CANYON PRESS TITLES,
PLEASE CALL 360-385-4925 EXT. 103

The Chinese character for poetry is made
up of two parts: "word" and "temple." It also
serves as pressmark for Copper Canyon Press.

The typefaces in this book were designed by
digital typography pioneers Carol Twombly
(text face Chaparral) and Zuzana Licko (dis-
play face Solex). Book design by VJB/Scribe.
Printed on archival-quality paper.